I first met Glen when he was on staff at LifeWay, leading the charge for Christian education. His passion for investing in the next generation is unequalled when it comes to teaching them to have a biblical worldview. Glen has mentored thousands of educators through the years. We were blessed to have Glen as our Headmaster at Sherwood Christian Academy, and his influence is still felt today. He took a school that didn't really know or fully understand its purpose and shaped and refined it on every level, from curriculum to faculty. You hold in your hands a valuable resource to put you on the path to a better tomorrow for your home, church, or school. If you want to take the next generation to the next level, learn the principles of Kingdom Education.

Dr. Michael Catt,
Retired Pastor
Sherwood Baptist Church,
Albany, GA

Understanding
Kingdom
Education™

A Challenge for the Home,
Church, and School

Glen Schultz

Understanding Kingdom Education™
A Challenge for the Home, Church, and School

© 2021 by Glen Schultz

Published by Wheaton Press
Wheaton, Illinois
www.WheatonPress.com

ISBN-10: 1-950258-39-4
ISBN-13: 978-1-950258-39-0 (WheatonPress.com)

Scripture taken from the New King James Version®. Copyright © 1982 by Thomas Nelson. Used by permission. All rights reserved.

Go to www.WheatonPress.com to learn about additional resources.

In memory of Dr. Paul Kienel.

Dr. Kienel modeled what it is to be a kingdom-focused husband, father, and educator. His encouragement over the years provided me with the desire and determination to know and understand God's plan for educating future generations. Without his godly influence on my life, this book would not be a reality.

Contents

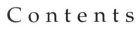

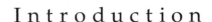

Introduction

IT HAS BEEN MORE THAN 50 YEARS AGO that I first walked into a high school chemistry classroom to begin my career in education. Throughout this time, I have had an unquenchable thirst to understand what education is all about from a biblical perspective. This thirst for understanding education from God's perspective has led me to dig deep into Scripture and read so many books on the subject that I lost count a long time ago.

When I left secular education and entered the field of Christian education, I found myself trying to understand what the real difference was between the two. I found that teachers were doing some of the same things in the same ways I had done during my five years in secular schools. There had to be more to this thing we call education than what I was seeing.

While serving as superintendent at Lynchburg Christian Academy, I began to develop a biblical philosophy of education. I sat under the teaching of some of the giants of the modern Christian day school movement. Dr. Roy Lowrie, Jr, Dr. Paul Kienel, Dr. Tony Fortosis,

Reverend Gene Garrick, Bud Schindler, Dr. Ron Chadwick, and others challenged me to rethink education from a biblical worldview. Little did I know what God had in store for me.

Having entered the field of education without any formal training was both challenging and rewarding at the same time. I hadn't been taught to think of education from a secular point of view. Therefore, I was able to begin developing my thoughts about the purpose of education without the baggage that comes from being indoctrinated by the typical departments of education grounded in secular thought.

As I began sharing what God was teaching me about education with others, I sensed that those listening had a hunger for truth much like my own. In 1996, I accepted a position with LifeWay Christian Resources to head up their new assignment in Christian schools and homeschooling. I was surprised to find that very few people at LifeWay understood Christian schooling and even fewer supported it in any way.

I quickly got the sense that most people there expected me to come in and cram Christian schools or homeschools down everyone's throat. However, I simply started sharing what God had been teaching me about what the Bible says about education. Soon, other leaders at LifeWay shared with me that they believed the same things I was sharing. One day, I was told that I needed to put what I was teaching in writing.

Even though I never envisioned writing a book, I was now tasked with this assignment. In 1998, *Kingdom Education: God's Plan for Educating Future Generations* was published. From that time forward, the message of Kingdom Education™ has become my life's work.

A second edition was released in 2002, and specific biblical principles detailing Kingdom Education™ were developed; for 18 years, Dr. Larry Taylor and I conducted an annual Kingdom School Institute, and hundreds, if not thousands, of parents, church leaders, and educators have read the book. I have been absolutely amazed by how the two simple words, "Kingdom Education," have taken hold in homes, churches, and schools.

Today, Kingdom Education™ is a buzzword in the Christian school movement. I have come across schools that publicly state they are Kingdom Education™ schools. Individuals identify themselves as leaders in Kingdom Education™. Organizations use the phrase "Kingdom education" to identify much of their work. This is very exciting but concerning at the same time. Even though the words "Kingdom education" are being trumpeted by individuals and organizations more and more, do they really understand its meaning, and are they fully implementing it?

For me, my thirst and hunger to fully understand God's plan for educating future generations remain unquenched. My understanding of Kingdom Education™ has deepened in ways I can't explain, from the time the book was first released. I have been asked if I was going to revise *Kingdom Education* with all that I have learned over the past 20+ years. I still believe that the original work lays a solid foundation for people to begin to understand God's plan for educating future generations.

After much thought and prayer, God has led me to write *Understanding Kingdom Education: A Challenge to the Home, Church and School*. This book is written to complement my book, *Kingdom Education: God's*

Plan for Educating Future Generations. In that book, I present the foundational principles that make up a biblical philosophy of education. This book is not meant to be a revision of my first book. Rather, I believed that there needed to be something that would guide Christians on taking "the next step" in understanding how God wants us to educate our children and youth.

Since this book is about education, it is important that each person reading it takes some time to answer a simple question: *How do you define education?* So, stop reading, take out a piece of paper or your electronic device, and write out how you would define the term "education." If you are able to do so, share your definition with another person or with your group.

Everyone talks a great deal about education. However, when asked to define the word, many people struggle to do so. When I have done this in a group setting, I ask the participants to share their definitions; amazingly, I have yet to have two people write down the exact same definition for this term.

It is even true when I do this exercise with faculty at a school. In those cases, everyone is teaching at the same school, yet there are as many definitions of the word as there are people in the audience. A common response I receive when asking this question goes something like this: "I know what it is, but I don't know how to put it into words."

Let me ask you a second question. Did you define education, or did you define "schooling"? It is fascinating to discover that when most people hear the word "education," they immediately think of schooling. It is true that schooling makes up a major portion of education, but it is only one part of a very complex process.

It is my prayer that you will not only be able to correctly define the word "education" by the time you finish this book, but you will also understand it from a biblical perspective. That is the challenge I want to present to you as you get ready to pursue God's meaning and purpose for education.

I trust you will be challenged and encouraged as you take the journey to understanding Kingdom Education™. We begin by looking at the importance of "The Book"!

Chapter 1

"The Book"

"The secret of my success: It is simple.
It is found in the Bible."[1]
GEORGE WASHINGTON CARVER

MY FATHER WAS A VERY PRINCIPLED MAN. His life was marked by discipline and hard work. He lived such a life, even though he suffered from severe arthritis and psoriasis for most of his adult life. I cannot remember him being able to walk any long distance or do any type of physical exercise without experiencing great pain. However, I never heard him complain and, through all of these struggles, he exhibited an unbelievable work ethic.

Dad was a man who unceasingly served others and never wanted to receive credit for his efforts. He was a member of the trustee board at

---

1   George Washington Carver. AZQuotes.com, Wind and Fly LTD, 2021.
    https://www.azquotes.com/quote/698124, accessed 2021.

his local church and served as the chairman of the building committee when the church was moving to a new location. Yet, through all of this, he was never out in the public but always quietly working behind the scenes.

Having lost his father when he was only 12 years old probably played a large role in the development of his demanding work ethic and his strong sense of personal responsibility and accountability. Dad had to learn to work hard to help support his mother and two sisters. I am convinced that he was able to accomplish all he did under difficult circumstances because he took his faith very seriously.

Three character qualities always stood out to everyone who knew Dad. The first was his punctuality. My father loathed people who were always late for appointments and/or completing tasks assigned to them. In fact, I have always characterized my father as one who considered himself to be "late" if he was less than 30 minutes early to anything.

A second quality found in Dad was his unwavering sense of loyalty. He was loyal to his family, friends, church, community, and workplace. He missed very few of my brother's and my basketball games in high school, and I learned he used most of his vacation time at work to travel to see me play college ball.

Dad worked for only two companies his entire life after completing junior college. After 16 years at Loblaws (a now-defunct grocery chain in Buffalo), he went to work for the National Grinding Wheel Company. He remained there for the next 41 years before retiring. As I think back on those years, I cannot recall a single day that my father ever missed work because of sickness.

Another area of his life where Dad demonstrated loyalty related to his church. He was always in attendance for services on Sundays and Wednesday nights. I still remember "his pew" where our family faithfully sat for every service (of course, it was always available because we were always early). He always supported the man who was called to pastor the church. He not only supported but also defended our various pastors with the tenacity a mama bear has for her cubs.

I personally witnessed him slipping a $50 or $100 bill into one of his pastor's hands when he shook hands with him after a service. I once asked him why he did that. He simply said that he knew the pastor's family was struggling to make ends meet on the meager salary the church provided. He wanted to encourage him. This made a huge impression on me because we were not a wealthy family by any means.

The third character trait that stood out in my father's life was his strong conviction about being personally accountable for one's actions. He grew up in a day when right was right and wrong was wrong. Right and wrong were based on absolute moral values that most people believed in. When someone did something wrong, Dad expected and demanded that they take responsibility for their actions and accept the consequences that came with the offense. I don't need to tell you that this conviction was demonstrated often as he disciplined his three children.

It was these three character traits – punctuality, loyalty, and accountability – that played themselves out in a very real way in my father's life. This was never more evident than when Dad decided to serve the small town of Pendleton, New York, and was elected the town's justice of the peace. Dad served two terms as justice, and I had the distinct privilege to watch him in action, as most of his proceedings took place at our dining room table.

My father did not have any legal training, so he was constantly reading the books that contained the legal codes for the town, state, and country. When a case was brought before him, there was one thing that everyone involved soon understood. Dad always **"went by The Book"**! I cannot remember how many times he would warn me that if I ever came before him as Justice, he would go by the book. It was **The Book** that guided my dad's decisions as justice of the peace.

He would never go beyond his scope of authority as outlined by the law. However, he would do whatever the law allowed to see a life corrected and not merely punished. There was one case that stands out in my mind. A man had gotten angry and smashed his car with a sledgehammer one night. After breaking out the car's headlights, windows, etc., he drove it around in the dark and was arrested.

He and his wife had to appear before Dad. It turned out that the man already had a suspended license. Dad's sentence for the crime was unique but absolutely necessary. He revoked the man's license for a year and then sentenced him to *six months in church!* Yes, you read it right. Dad knew the man had a spiritual problem, so he required him to attend a church (didn't matter which one) every Sunday for six months. He had to submit an affidavit signed by the pastor of the church that this person had attended his church each Sunday. As you can see, Dad *went by The Book!*

I wanted to start this book out by telling you about my father because of how Dad lived his life **by The Book!** Education plays a huge role in the lives of our children and youth. The education a child receives will not only affect his or her own life, but it will also affect the culture of society. If the home, church, and school are going to raise a generation of young people who can impact their world for the Lord, everyone must educate their children **by The Book!**

Dad went by the books that contained the laws of the land when he served as justice of the peace. However, I am not talking about merely going by the books that contain the laws of one's country or community. Christian parents, church leaders, and educators must go by **The Book.** This book is the Bible, God's Word. God's Word is the only source where people can find and receive direction on how God wants them to educate a child. I have long been convinced that the only way we are going to reverse the terrible condition we find ourselves in today is for Christians to **go by The Book!**

However, Christians can never **go by The Book** if they don't know **The Book**. One will not know **The Book** if they seldom spend time in **The Book**. As a former chemistry teacher, I am very familiar with Robert Boyle, the scientist who formulated Boyle's law of gases. However, Boyle was in **The Book** for guidance in his work. Here is what Boyle had to say about **The Book**.

> *The Bible is indeed among books what the diamond is among precious stones.*

In the Bible, the ignorant may learn all requisite knowledge, and the most knowing may learn to discern their ignorance.[2]

I use the Scriptures, not as an arsenal to be resorted to only for arms and weapons but as a matchless temple, where I delight to be, to contemplate the beauty, the symmetry, and the magnificence of the structure and to increase my awe and excite my devotion to the Deity there preached and adored.[3]

Boyle was not the only person who understood how important it was to know what the Bible says and, therefore, spent time daily studying and meditating on it. Consider the following examples.

The Bible is God's chart for you to steer by, to keep you from the bottom of the sea, to show you where the harbour is, and how to reach it without running on rocks and bars.[4]

Henry Ward Beecher

---

2   Robert Boyle. AZQuotes.com, Wind and Fly LTD, 2021. https://www.azquotes.com/quote/1181519, accessed 2021.

3   Robert Boyle. AZQuotes.com, Wind and Fly LTD, 2021. https://www.azquotes.com/quote/1181520, accessed 2021.

4   Josiah Hotchkiss Gilbert, *Dictionary of Burning Words of Brilliant Writers.* (New York: W.B. Ketcham, 1895), 28, https://archive.org/details/dictionaryburni00gilbgoog/page/n40/mode/2up.

I have come to the decision that the Bible is a supernatural book, that it has come from God, and that the only safety for the human race is to follow its teachings.[5]

Salmon P. Chase

Do you know a book that you are willing to put under your head for a pillow when you are dying? Very well; that is the book you want to study when you are living. There is only one such book in the world – The Bible.[6]

Joseph Cook

After more than 60 years of almost daily reading of the Bible, I never fail to find it always new and marvelously in tune with the changing needs of every day.[7]

Cecil B. DeMille

Most Christians in the United States own a Bible. Barna Group's research claims that almost 90% of American homes have a Bible available to them for study and meditation. However, in a 2017 study on the state of the Bible in America, Barna reported some sad findings. In this study, Kinnaman notes that *half of Americans are "Bible users" – that is, they engage with the Bible by reading, listening to, or praying with the Bible on their own at least **three to four times A YEAR!** (emphasis

---

5   Salmon P. Chase. AZQuotes.com, Wind and Fly LTD, 2021. https://www. azquotes.com/quote/1340304, accessed 2021.

6   Joseph Cook, *Orthodoxy: With Preludes on Current Events,* American edition. (D. Bryce and Son, 1878), https://archive.org/details/ orthodoxywithpr03cookgoog?ref=ol&view=theater .

7   Cecil B. DeMille. AZQuotes.com, Wind and Fly LTD, 2021. https://www. azquotes.com/quote/1249508, accessed 2021.

mine) A "Bible user" is one who engages with the living Word of God only three to four times a year!

The report went on to state that *most Americans esteem the Bible and have access to it. However, even if there's a baseline of respect, people aren't sure how to apply the lessons of Scripture to public life or society, particularly in an increasingly pluralistic nation.* Unfortunately, these findings give evidence to what many Christian leaders have said for quite some time. Today's church is one of the most biblically illiterate people in New Testament church history.

D. Martyn Lloyd-Jones challenged the church of his day to choose what its members were going to do with respect to the Bible's authority in their lives. The questions he posed to Christians in the early to mid-20th century need to be heeded by today's parents, church leaders, and educators.

> *We all, therefore, have to face this ultimate and final question: Do we accept the Bible as the Word of God, as the sole authority in all matters of faith and practice, or do we not? Is the whole of my thinking governed by Scripture, or do I come with my reason and pick and choose out of Scripture and sit in judgment upon it, putting myself and modern knowledge forward as the ultimate standard and authority? The issue is crystal clear. Do I accept Scripture as a revelation from God, or do I trust human understanding and human reasons? Or, putting it still more simply, do I pin my faith to, and subject all my thinking to, what I read in the Bible? Or do I defer to modern knowledge, to modern learning, to what people think today, to what we*

know at this present time that was not known in the past?
It is inevitable that we occupy one or the other of those two
positions.[8]

I am becoming more and more convinced that every Christian goes through what I refer to as a *crisis of faith*. It is at this point in one's life they must make a decision like Lloyd-Jones set before Christians of his day. At one time, the main battle for the Bible was for its inerrancy. The big question – is the Bible without error? – was at the center of the battle. Biblical inerrancy is summed up in the words of Bible scholar, J. Otis Yoder.

> *Biblical inerrancy means the Bible contains no error. It*
> *is without error in faith and fact. If we have the self-*
> *disclosure of the holy God, it cannot be mixed with error.*
> *Error and truth cannot be contained in the same document*
> *that claims to be a self-disclosure of a holy, righteous God.*
> *If error is mixed with truth, then that is deception, which*
> *violates the character of God.*[9]

Today, the battle has taken on greater significance. Not only must every Christian decide whether or not the Bible is true but also whether it is sufficient. John Piper explains the sufficiency of Scripture this way:

---

8 R. Albert Mohler, Jr. 2005. *D. Martyn Lloyd-Jones on the Authority of Scripture—We Must Choose Between Two Positions.* June 19. Accessed 2021. https://albertmohler.com/2005/06/19/d-martyn-lloyd-jones-on-the-authority-of-scripture-we-must-choose-between-two-positions.

9 J. Otis Yoder & Harold S. Martin, *Biblical Inerrancy and Reliability.* (Harrisonburg, VA: Fellowship of Concerned Mennonites, 1985).

*We don't need any more inspired, inerrant words. In the
Bible God has given us, we have the perfect standard for
judging all other knowledge.*[10]

Chuck Swindoll makes it clear Christians must believe that the Bible is
God's Word and, therefore, it is without error and sufficient in and of
itself to guide us in how to live our lives.

*The Bible **is** the authority, the final resting place of our cares,
our worries, our griefs, our tragedies, our sorrows, and our
surprises. It is the final answer to our questions, our search.
Turning back to the Scriptures will provide something that
nothing else on the entire earth can provide.*[11]

Christians memorize many important verses in the Bible but fail to
understand the deep meaning of the words in those verses. Being in
and studying **The Book** are major themes found throughout Scripture.
A few of these passages come to my mind:

*This Book of the Law shall not depart from your mouth,
but you shall meditate in it day and night, that you may
observe to do according to all that is written in it. For then
you will make your way prosperous, and then you will have
good success.*

Joshua 1:8

---

10   John Piper, "Thoughts on the sufficiency of Scripture: What It Does and
Doesn't Mean," Desiring God, February 9, 2005, www.desiringgod.org/
articles/thoughts-on-the-sufficiency-of-scripture

11   Charles Swindoll, *Growing Deep in the Christian Life: Returning to Our Roots.*
(Portland, OR: Multnomah Press, 1986), 56 .

With my whole heart I have sought You; Oh, let me not wander from Your commandments! Your Word I have hidden in my heart, that I might not sin against You.

Psalm 119:10-11

But He answered and said, "It is written, 'Man shall not live by bread alone, but by every word that proceeds from the mouth of God.'"

Matthew 4:4

If you abide in My word, you are My disciples indeed. And you shall know the truth, and the truth shall make you free...If you abide in Me, and My words abide in you, you will ask what you desire, and it shall be done for you.

John 8:31-32; 15:7

All Scripture is given by inspiration of God and is profitable for doctrine (what's right), for reproof (what's wrong), for correction (how to get right), for instruction in righteousness (how to stay right), that the man of God may be complete, thoroughly equipped for every good work.

2 Timothy 3:16-17

For the Word of God is living and powerful, and sharper than any two-edged sword, piercing even to the division of soul and spirit, and of joints and marrow, and is a discerner of the thoughts and intents of the heart.

Hebrews 4:12

If a Christian parent, church leader, or educator is not willing to go by **The Book**, he or she will never know how God intends for us to educate our children. Before you read any further in this book, I challenge you to come to the conviction that John Wesley had about **The Book**. Wesley said this about **The Book:**

> *My ground is the Bible. Yea, I am a Bible-bigot. I follow it in all things, both great and small.*[12]

It is time for the church, the body of Christ, to **address the issue of education biblically!**

---

12 Wesley, John. 2019. QuoteTab. Accessed 2021. http://quotetab.com/quote/by-john-wesley/my-ground-is-the-bible-yea-i-am-a-bible-bigot-i-follow-it-in-all-things-both?source=bigots .

Chapter 2

Defining Education

"The end of education is to repair the ruins
of our first parents: to know God, to love
Him, to be like Him, to imitate Him."[13]
JOHN MILTON

EDUCATION IS DEFINITELY A HOT TOPIC in today's world. Every parent wants his or her child to receive a "good education." Education is seen as the cure-all for each and every social ill. In fact, Satan is still tempting man with the same lie but using a different tree than he used on Adam and Eve in Genesis 3.

---

13 John Milton, "Of Education," in *Basic Writings in Christian Education,* ed. Kendig Brubaker Cully. (Philadelphia: Westminster Press, 1960) 24.

If you recall, Satan tempted man in the garden by telling them if they ate of the Tree of Knowledge of Good and Evil, they would become perfect. They would be "like God." Of course, we all know the disastrous results that have occurred because our original parents believed Satan's lie.

Today, he is still at it, trying to get mankind to be "like God" by eating of a certain tree. He tempts us with the lie that if we would only eat of a certain tree, we would solve all of life's problems – we would become perfect. The tree Satan is using today is the *tree of education*.

If we listen to what is being put forth today, this seduction is clearly seen. Think of what society's solution to poverty is. Education. What is the cure for the teenage pregnancy problem? Sex education. How do we overcome alcohol and drug addiction? Drug education. We only need to *eat of the tree of education* and we will solve all of our problems. If the education we are giving our children isn't doing this, we need to simply pour more money, resources, and efforts into improving education. In the end, education will solve every social ill and inequality.

In order to *address the issue of education biblically*, one must first understand what education is. In the introduction, I asked you to take a few minutes and define education on a piece of paper. As I explained earlier, I have done this with a lot of people over the past several years of speaking and consulting. I find it fascinating that everyone talks about education, but when it comes to defining it, they struggle to do so.

It bears repeating that to most people, including Christians, education is mainly equated with "schooling." If you ask a parent if he or she wants their child to receive a good education, the parent will quickly say "yes."

Then, the parent will describe what kind of school he or she believes can provide the child with a good education.

The Merriam-Webster Dictionary gives the following definitions of education:

> *The action or process of teaching someone, especially in school, college, or university; the knowledge, skill, understanding that you get from attending a school, college, or university*[14]

If we look at the derivation of the term "educate," we will find two ideas put forth. The first comes from the Latin word *educare*. This word means 'bring up," "to rise," and "to nourish." The second comes from the Latin word *educere*. This word means "to lead out," "to draw out," and "to bring from." Both of these terms related to education indicate that there is something that needs to be instilled in every person and that the process of education must nurture or draw out something in the person.

When I refer to education, I am referring to something multi-faceted. Schooling plays a huge role in this process. However, schooling cannot be equated with education. Schooling is only a part of education. What takes place in the home and the church are also parts of the educational process or effort.

Unfortunately, most Christians have wasted time and energy debating the wrong things when it comes to how we are to educate our children.

---

14   "Education." *Merriam-Webster.com Dictionary,* Merriam-Webster, https://www.merriam-webster.com/dictionary/education. Accessed 1 Jun. 2021.

Christians have debated where children should go to school, for example, which has proven very detrimental to the actual education our children have received. This is because when the debate is about where children ought to go to school, education has been relegated to schooling only.

Christians must understand that education is the total process of nurturing, instructing, bringing up, teaching, guiding, training, etc. our children at home, church, and school. Some people might argue that we must also include the media and peers as parts of the educational process. My response is that the home should be determining and structuring the media's and peers' influences on the education the child receives.

So, how can we accurately define education? Let me share three definitions with you that I hope will help clarify what education really means.

A Secular Definition

If someone were to take a university course in the foundations of education, they might find a definition of education to be something like this.

> *Education is the formal and informal process of instilling knowledge, skills, and understanding in a child that will prepare them to be successful adults in today's world.*

In fact, this may be the most common understanding parents have when they state the desire that their children get a good education. What they are saying is that they want their children to know the right stuff to get into a good college so that they will be equipped with the right stuff to get a good job. The reason I have labeled this a "secular" definition is that it is devoid of any spiritual meaning.

This definition is completely temporal in scope and primarily deals with the child's mind and maybe some physical skills. It is focused almost entirely on knowing facts and the use of those facts to be successful in life – and life is only viewed from a temporal, earthly existence.

A Biblical Definition

Kevin Swanson gives a much broader definition of education in his book, *Upgrade: 10 Secrets to the Best Education for Your Child*. Swanson defines education as:

> *The preparation of a child intellectually, emotionally, spiritually, and physically for life and for eternity.*[15]

Swanson defines education as a process of preparing children for something in the future. Yes, the author believes every child needs to be prepared for life here on earth. However, he also understands that this life is only a precursor to real life – a life that will go on into eternity.

The preparation of a child must involve the whole child. It must develop the child's mind, body, emotions, and spirit. I would also suggest that

---

15   Kevin Swanson, *Upgrade: 10 Secrets to the Best Education for Your Child.*
     (Nashville TN: B&H Publishers, 2006), 10.

developing a child socially should be included. This addition would define education as:

> *The preparation of a child intellectually, emotionally, spiritually, physically, and socially for life and eternity.*

I do believe this is a "biblical" definition, as it follows the pattern of Jesus' education as described in Luke 2:52. When Jesus was 12 years old, He was in the temple questioning the religious leaders of His day. After this, we do not know anything about his life until he enters his adult ministry. What we do know from Scripture is that Jesus went home with His parents and He was "educated," as described in this verse. I have connected the Scripture with this definition of education.

> *And Jesus increased in wisdom* (intellectually) *and stature* (physically) *and in favor with God* (spiritually) *and men* (socially).
>
> Luke 2:52

Another Biblical Definition

I have always had a passion to discover and understand God's purpose for education. In studying the Scriptures, I realized that to understand God's purpose for education, I had to first understand the purpose for man's existence. To understand this required understanding God's purpose for why anything and everything exists. Without this fundamental understanding of why everything and anything exists, it is impossible to fully comprehend God's intended purpose for education.

There is a meta-narrative in Scripture that unfolds God's purpose for His creation and gives man meaning for life. This meta-narrative is broken into several chapters: creation, the fall, redemption, restoration, and glorification. Studying the Bible's meta-narrative, or big picture, explains God's purpose for all things – including education.

God is eternal in both His person and His nature or character. He determined to express His magnificent glory by creating the universe. When you read Genesis 1, substitute the words, *Let there be* with *Here is who I am.* Creation is an expression of the very nature of God. This is the message we find in Psalm 19:1-7 and Romans 1:20.

Not only is creation an expression of who God is, but it also exists for one purpose – God's glory. Paul makes it clear that God is the ultimate end of creation when he wrote Colossians 1:16 and Romans 11:36. Everything exists *by Him* and *for Him.* Jonathan Edwards stated,

> *The end of creation is that creation might glorify [God}…*
> *the glory of God might be magnified in the universe.*[16]

Edwards understood that the created universe and all that it contains, including man, was to bring glory to God.

> *God made the world that He might communicate, and the*
> *creature receive, His glory and that it might be received*
> *both by the mind and heart…The Son of God created the*

---

16   Jonathan Edwards, quoted in John Piper, *God's Passion for His Glory.* (Wheaton, IL: Crossway Books, 1998), 32.

world for this very end, **to communicate Himself in an image of His own excellency.**[17]

On the sixth day of God's work of creation, God made man in His own image. By creating man in His image, God distinguishes man from the rest of creation. Man is the only created being with the capacity to study God's creation, see God in the creation, and give Him the glory that is due Him. As I studied Romans 1:20 and Psalm 19:1-7, it became apparent that education should lead a person to a greater understanding of who God is for the purpose of giving God glory. Therefore, I developed the following definition of education.

> *The study of God and His creation through which God reveals His nature to the learner so that the learner can know Him and give Him glory.*

I have shared this with various groups of parents and teachers and asked for their thoughts on this definition. Without exception, the pushback that I receive goes something like this: This definition is fine for science and Bible class, but what about the academics?

As you contemplated this definition of education, did you think the same thing? What that type of logic reveals is most Christians have a very narrow view of creation. Most of us think that creation is simply the physical matter that makes up the universe. Christians fail to realize that everything a person studies in school and/or life is part of God's creation. Albert Greene said it best when he wrote,

---

17   Jonathan Edwards, quoted in John Piper, 76, 79.

We must avoid the impression that academics represents the fullness of what school [education] is all about. Knowing God in and through the creation is what is important… It brings no honor to the Holy Spirit if we then proceed to treat the ordinary school studies, which are derived totally from the created world, as if they had nothing to do with God. They are laden with meaning because they are all part of God's way of giving Himself to us, of making Himself known to us.[18]

Christian parents, church leaders, and educators must abandon any temporal, secular understanding of what education is. Christians must also avoid equating education with schooling. The body of Christ must address the issue of education biblically and that begins by viewing education as a multi-faceted process that takes place in the home, the church, and school. We must define education as the all-inclusive effort of the home, church, and school to prepare future generations for life and eternity by studying God's creation in order to know Him, be like Him, and give Him glory.

---

18   Albert E. Greene, *Reclaiming the Future of Christian Education: A Transforming Vision.* (Colorado Springs, CO: ACSI, 1998), 37, 44.

Chapter 3

A Kingdom Mindset

"The seeking of the Kingdom of God is the chief business of the Christian life."[19]
JONATHAN EDWARDS

SINCE WRITING THE BOOK, *Kingdom Education: God's Plan for Educating Future Generations*, I have been asked on many occasions why I titled the book *Kingdom Education*? The answer needs some explanation.

At the time, I was serving the Lord at LifeWay Christian Resources and heading up the section dealing with Christian schools and

---

19 Edwards, Jonathan. n.d. *The Pastor's Workshop.* Accessed 2021. https://thepastorsworkshop.com/sermon-quotes-by-topic/sermon-quotes-kingdom-of-god/.

homeschooling. The leadership at LifeWay was putting forth a major emphasis on the importance of the Kingdom of God. Through listening to the various messaging taking place throughout LifeWay and my own personal study of the Word, I came to develop a profound conviction about the Kingdom of God.

The Kingdom of God is a major topic in the New Testament and is considered the central theme of Jesus' teachings. As historian Michael Grant puts it,

> *...every thought and saying of Jesus was directed and subordinated to one single thing...the realization of the Kingdom of God upon the earth. ...This one phrase [Kingdom of God] sums up his whole ministry and his whole life's work.*[20]

There are 86 references to the Kingdom of God, the Kingdom of Heaven, and other synonymous phrases/words in the gospels of Matthew, Mark, Luke, and John alone. The term "kingdom" had several meanings in Scripture. At times, it referred to a geographical territory. When a king divided his kingdom up, it was referring to the geographical territory the king ruled over.

Other times, the term "kingdom" referred to the millennial reign of Christ here on earth. Or it was associated with God's ultimate reign in Heaven for all of eternity. There is a battle between the kingdom of darkness and the kingdom of light going on here on earth. Satan offered Jesus the kingdoms on earth that he controlled.

---

20 *Jesus: An Historian's Review of the Gospels*, 1995, pp.10-11.

As I studied all these different meanings and concepts of the terms "kingdom" and the "Kingdom of God," I was convicted of the truth that God's highest priority for every Christian was to know, understand, and experience His Kingdom each and every day of his or her life. This conviction was based on Jesus' teaching in Matthew 5-7. Jesus concluded this lengthy lesson with the words found in Matthew 6:33, *But seek **first** His kingdom…*

Pastor James McMenis explains how important it is to make sure we seek God's Kingdom above everything else in life. He said,

> *Whatever or whoever you put first in your life controls every other aspect of your life.*[21]

Pastor and author Timothy Keller makes this point even more forcefully when he writes,

> *Whatever you live for actually owns you. You do not really control yourself. Whatever you live for and love the most controls you.*[22]

Most Christians have memorized this verse and will give a hearty "amen" to someone saying that Christians need to seek God's Kingdom above anything else we might seek in this life. However, the question that begs an answer is, *what is the Kingdom of God?* If we don't know the answer to this question, how can we know we are seeking His Kingdom

---

21   James McMenis, quoted by Glen Schultz in "Developing a Kingdom Mindset," Kingdom Education Ministries, January 21, 2008, https://kingdomeducationministries.com/2018/01/developing-a-kingdom-mindset.

22   Timothy J. Keller, *The Prodigal Prophet: Jonah and the Mystery of God's Mercy.* (New York, New York: Viking, 2018).

as the top priority in our lives? One must know what the Kingdom of God is if they are going to seek it.

We often hear theologians explain that the Kingdom of God is here right now but is yet to come or that His Kingdom is both inside and outside a person. These concepts of the Kingdom of God are true, but they don't clearly define what the Kingdom of God is.

Drs. Gene Mims and Ken Hemphill helped me understand this all-important concept in their books, *Thine is the Kingdom* and *EKG: Empowering Kingdom Growth*. Mims stated that the Kingdom of God is...

> *the reign of God through Jesus Christ in the life of a believer and is evidenced by God working in, through, and around the individual.*[23]

Mims' definition of the Kingdom of God made sense to me. The Kingdom of God is the authority and reign of God on earth and in Heaven. This new understanding helped me have a better grasp of Jesus' teaching on prayer when He told His disciples to ask that *Thy will be done on earth as it is in Heaven.*

God's will is done to perfection in Heaven, and He wants His will to be done here on earth the same way – through complete obedience to His commands. In other words, the Kingdom of God is present wherever and whenever His will is done. This means I experience His Kingdom to the degree I obey His will. This won't happen if God is not reigning

---

23   Gene Mims, *Thine is the Kingdom.* (Nashville: LifeWay Press, 1997), 18.

in each and every Christian's life. I now understand God wants to reign in my life completely.

Hemphill clarified the meaning of the Kingdom of God for me when he explained the Kingdom this way. He wrote that one couldn't have a kingdom if he is not a king. One cannot be a king unless he has subjects under him. So, the Kingdom of God is simply the reality of God being king over His subjects. As king, He sets the rules, and His subjects obey them. John Stott captures this thought best when he writes,

> *Greatness in the Kingdom of God is measured in terms of obedience.*[24]

The Kingdom of God is the rule and reign of God in the lives of believers. When God rules and reigns in the lives of believers, they can be used to extend His Kingdom rule in the lives of others. As we develop a Kingdom mindset, we will be obedient to the will of God individually and corporately. Hemphill says,

> *Simply put, a kingdom enterprise is where the power of God is evident, the presence of God is experienced, and the purposes of God are realized.*[25]

Disciple Nations Alliance (DNA) identifies four essential ingredients that must exist for any kingdom to exist. These four essentials are:

---

24 John Stott, *Authentic Christianity,* ed. Timothy Dudley-Smith. (InterVarsity Press, 1995).

25 Ken Hemphill, "Introduction," in *EKG: Empowering Kingdom Growth,* second edition. (Nashville: B&H Academic, 2010).

- There must be a king who rules.
- There must be subjects the king rules.
- There must be laws or ordinances by which the king rules.
- There must be a territory over which a king rules.[26]

When one applies these truths to the Kingdom of God, it looks like this.

- God is the king.
- Christians are the subjects the king rules.
- God's Word, the Bible, contains the laws and ordinances by which the king rules.
- A Christian's life – mind, will, emotions – is the territory over which the king rules.

God explained to Moses why He chose Israel to be His people in order to advance His Kingdom in the world.

> *You have seen what I did to the Egyptians and how I bore you on eagles' wings and brought you to Myself. Now, therefore, if you will indeed obey My voice and keep My covenant, then you shall be a special treasure to Me above all people; for all the earth is Mine. And you shall be to Me a kingdom of priests and a holy nation. These are the words which you shall speak to the children of Israel.*
>
> Exodus 19:4-6

This same declaration was made by David when he became king of Israel. David had developed a Kingdom mindset.

---

26   Coram Deo and A School for Discipling Nations. 2021. *The Basics Course.*

Therefore, You are great, O Lord God. For there is none like You, nor is there any God besides You, according to all that we have heard with our ears. And who is like Your people, like Israel, the one nation on the earth whom God went to redeem for Himself as a people, to make for Himself a name—and to do for Yourself great and awesome deeds for Your land—before Your people whom You redeemed for Yourself from Egypt, the nations, and their gods?

2 Samuel 7:22-23

We must ask ourselves a few questions to determine if we have a Kingdom mindset.

1. What is your passion?
2. What is your purpose?
3. What motivates you?

According to Hemphill, God is seeking a people who will:

- Embody His name
- Embrace His mission
- Obey His Word

Are we motivated by the kingdoms of this world that only result in the applause of men? Or, are we motivated by a passion for the Kingdom of God, which will always result in the reward of the Father? If Christians develop a Kingdom mindset, they will be people who *know the King and will serve Him!* When this takes place in our lives, *revelation will rule over human reason!*

With this understanding of what the Kingdom of God is and the priority it must have in every Christian's life, I was able to write about a Kingdom mindset regarding education. I was convicted that God wanted to reign completely in every Christian's life. That meant He wanted to reign in a Christian's home, church, vocation, and even the education one gives to future generations.

So, when I present *Kingdom Education*™, I am talking about the multi-faceted process of preparing future generations for life and eternity in which God reigns supreme. If God doesn't reign as king in the educational process, it is not Kingdom Education™. He doesn't reign as king in this process if His subjects don't obey His instructions on how to educate future generations.

The formal definition of Kingdom Education™ that is presented in my first book is as follows:

> *Kingdom Education*™ *is the life-long, Bible-based, Christ-centered process of*
> > *Leading a child to Christ,*
> > *Building a child up in Christ*
> > *Equipping a child to serve Christ*

This definition of Kingdom Education™ presents Christians with several fundamental principles of true education from God's perspective. The first principle is that Kingdom Education™ is a lifelong process. The second principle demands that God's Word be the foundation of all education. The final principle found in this definition is that Christ must be central in the entire educational process. Each of these principles will be developed in greater depth in later chapters.

We also can see that these principles of education are built on two pillars – the pillars of evangelism and discipleship. When one has a Kingdom mindset regarding how they educate a child, it becomes apparent that the gospel must be central to all aspects of a child's education. What good would it be if an individual were to become highly educated and never come to know Jesus Christ as his or her personal Savior? This understanding of education also means that only teachers who have experienced God's gift of eternal life can teach children the fundamental message of the gospel.

Some will argue that evangelism and discipleship are "church" responsibilities and are not what education, especially schooling, is all about. However, this argument only demonstrates that today's Christian has a limited understanding of biblical discipleship.

We must understand that Kingdom Education™ does not stop once a person comes to Christ. Once a child is saved, it is then necessary to build the child up in Christ. Paul referred to this principle in Colossians 2:7 when he wrote that it is important to be *rooted and built up in Him and established in the faith.* Immediately following this verse, Paul warned Christians to beware and not be ruined by philosophies and empty teaching based on the traditions of this world and not on the principles of Christ.

In order for a child to be rooted in Christ, we must understand several factors. First, we must recognize that each child is a unique creation of God. Psalm 139 is a marvelous passage of Scripture showing us that each person has been specially designed by the Master Creator, God Himself. This means every child will have special gifts or talents. True education recognizes these gifts and is designed to develop each talent to the fullest.

As a father of three, I quickly learned how God had designed my two sons and my daughter with unique abilities. One was very analytical. Another was more strong-willed but extremely creative. The third child was gifted with strong relational skills. Each one learned according to a different learning style, and we, as their parents, had to make sure we were building them up in Christ according to these gifts and talents.

Therefore, biblical discipleship occurs as an individual comes to know Christ as their personal Savior and then is taught to obey all of God's commands. This requires that the child knows his or her unique gifts from God and their unique calling from God to serve Him and impact God's Kingdom. As education takes a child and hones their God-given talents and abilities to their fullest, that child becomes equipped to serve Christ.

This definition also provides Christians with one goal of education they should have for all their children. The goal presented here is that our children should be equipped to serve Christ. This goal of Kingdom Education™ needs to be a driving force in everything the home, church, and school does when educating future generations. Our children should be prepared physically, intellectually, spiritually, emotionally, and socially to serve their Savior in this life as mature Christ-followers.

Since developing this definition, God has led me to understand what His ultimate end for His creation – including His ultimate end for all of mankind – is. Everything was created so He would be seen, known, and glorified throughout His creation.

With this in mind, I began asking myself the question, *why do we want our children to serve Christ?* Is serving Christ the ultimate goal of Kingdom Education™? Or is serving Christ something we do as a means to reach a higher calling or end? This new understanding of man's purpose has caused me to expand the original formal definition of Kingdom Education™. It now reads,

> *Kingdom Education™ is the lifelong, Bible-based, Christ-centered process of*
> > *Leading a child to Christ,*
> > *Building a child up in Christ*
> > *Equipping a child to serve Christ*
> > **Causing the child to know God and give Him glory!**

Putting all of this together will give us a better understanding of what God expects us to know about education. Education is a multi-faceted process involving the home, church, and school that prepares the whole child for life and eternity.

This preparation is accomplished when the home, church, and school guide the child through a study of God and His creation in an effort to cause the child to know God and bring Him glory in all the child will become and do in life. This will only happen when God reigns in the entire educational process – in the home, the church, and the school.

Understanding the Kingdom of God is necessary for parents, church leaders, and educators to be able to address the issue of education. The challenge all Christians face is knowing what God's instructions are for how He expects us to educate future generations. This is because these instructions must guide the entire educational process.

Our children need a foundation that is unchanging and consistent, regardless of where the training is taking place. When Kingdom Education™ becomes a reality in a child's life, the home, the church, and the school will build real meaning and purpose in each life, and future generations will once again have hope. To discover and obey these instructions, we must turn to "The Book" – God's Word!

Chapter 4

Avoiding Stubbing One's Toe

"An army of principles can penetrate where an army of soldiers cannot."[27]
THOMAS PAINE

I WANT YOU TO IMAGINE you are awakened out of a deep sleep by a noise you hear downstairs in your home. You know that you have to check it out, but you don't want to wake the family up. So, you try to get out of bed and make your way out of the bedroom, down the stairs, and through the various rooms. You do this without

---

27   Thomas Paine, *Common Sense, The Rights of Man, and Other Essential Writings of Thomas Payne.* (New York, New York: Classic House Books, 2009).

turning any lights on because you don't want to scare off a possible intruder nor do you want to disturb your wife and children as they sleep.

As you grope through the darkness, you discover that your wife rearranged some furniture that day. You make this painful discovery when you take a step and your small toe takes a sharp right turn around a table leg that was recently placed in your path. You end up screaming in pain as you stub your toe – and, of course, you wake up your entire family. Can you mentally feel the pain that only comes from a good stubbing of one's toe?

To avoid future stubbing of your toes when walking through a dark house, you come up with a couple of solutions. One is that you can keep all the lights on in the house. You quickly dismiss that option because you are one who cannot sleep with lights on.

A second option makes the best sense. You can purchase a few small nightlights that you can strategically place around the house where some dangerous, toe-stubbing objects are located. Those nightlights will let you know where danger is located, and you can avoid stubbing your toes. I want to take this analogy and apply it to avoiding stubbing our spiritual toes when it comes to educating future generations.

I was preparing a series of chapel services at the school I was leading a few years ago. I desired to help the students and faculty know how to make the right choices in every area of their lives. In order to do this, I secured the help of our youth pastor and began preparing the chapels.

Instead of preaching to the students on making right decisions, I chose to sit at a café table with the youth pastor. We would carry on a conversation on this topic, and the students and faculty would listen in. I met with the youth pastor, and we scripted the first chapel session. I set it up where the pastor would ask me a question that I believed would resonate and capture the attention of every student and faculty member. The youth pastor said the following to me:

> *I know that it is important to make the right decisions in all of life. I understand that every decision carries with it consequences that are either good or bad. I don't have a problem making the right decisions in areas where the Bible gives me specific commands – don't kill, steal, or covet. But here is where I struggle. How can I be sure that I am making the right decision in areas of my life **where the Bible is silent?***

When the youth pastor asked that question, everyone in the room leaned in to hear the answer. This is a question that every Christian has had to wrestle with at some time or another. My response was also captivating to the audience. I said,

> *If there is any area of life in which the Bible is silent, then you can do whatever you want to because God must not understand that area of your life!*

A hush fell over the room as my words sunk into their minds. The youth pastor looked at me and said that the Bible was written thousands of years ago. At the time, there was no internet, movies, Snapchat, Facebook, Instagram, etc. around. So, if the Bible is silent when it comes to these things, I can do with them anything I want to. My response was, *yes, if the Bible is silent about them.*

The key to making right decisions is understanding whether or not the Bible, God's Word, is silent about some areas of life. We must embrace the fact that God understands everything about all of life and, therefore, the Bible is not silent on *any* issue we might face.

Indeed, God does not give us specific commands one can apply to every area of life in the 21st century. If He had to do this, it would require a Bible that would be so long it would extend miles up into the atmosphere. However, God's Word not only has specific commands that we are to obey, but He also included biblical principles that would guide Christians in everyday decisions.

Let's consider the following verse.

> *Your Word is a lamp to my feet*
> *And a light to my path.*
>
> Psalm 119:105

I believe this verse explains how God's Word provides Christians with clear direction on how to make the right decisions in every area of life – including the education of future generations. I want to look at two types of light mentioned in this verse.

The first type of light I want you to focus on is a *light to my path.* Today, many of our roads have streetlights on them. These lights light the entire road or path. Even most houses have spotlights on their corners that, when turned on, light up a whole area of the yard. These *lights to our path* are bright and give us clear direction.

God's Word is described as being spotlights on our spiritual paths. These lights found in Scripture are God's commands. They are bright and give us clear direction. Whenever God tells us to **do** something or **don't do** something, there is no question what decision we are to make. Prime examples of these types of lights to our paths are the 10 Commandments.

The second type of light God's Word provides Christians is described as *lamps to my feet*. I learned that travelers in Bible times actually put small candles of some type on their sandals to be able to make their way when walking someplace in the night. These lamps to their feet did not light up the whole path, only what was directly in front of their feet.

This type of light is much like the nightlights we talked about earlier in this chapter. We can place them around our houses so that we won't stub our toes at night. These *lamps to my feet* represent biblical principles. Biblical principles make the Bible relevant regardless of:

- Circumstances
- Historical periods of time
- Society or cultural tendencies

The reason biblical principles ensure the relevancy of Scripture is that they are:

- Of an eternal nature
- As much God's Word (light) as His commands

Let's look at an example of how one biblical principle can offer direction on making right decisions in several areas of one's life. I refer to this principle as the *body principle*. There are numerous references in the Bible that tell Christians their bodies are temples where the Holy Spirit resides. Probably the most familiar of these Scripture references is 1 Corinthians 6:19-20, which reads,

> *Or do you not know that your body is the temple of the Holy Spirit who is in you, whom you have from God, and you are not your own? For you were bought with a price; therefore, glorify God in your body and in your spirit, which are God's.*

Here, we find God instructing us that we have been bought with a price, so we are not our own. Even our physical bodies now belong to God and, therefore, we are to glorify God in our bodies and our spirits or attitudes.

The figure on the next page illustrates the *body principle*.

This principle gives us guidance in deciding how we are to glorify God in our bodies. It can be applied to the four areas of our lives pictured on the next page:

- What we *put into* our bodies
- What *comes out* of our bodies
- What we *put on* our bodies
- What we *do with* our bodies

Your Body - God's Temple

What You Put On

What You Put In

What You Put Out

What You Do With

The Body Principle:
Does This Harm God's Temple?
Will It Glorify God?

Here is one simple principle – glorify God with your body – that guides us on what we eat and/or drink or listen to or watch or anything else we might put into our bodies, the words and attitudes that come out of our bodies, the clothes and other adornments we put on our bodies, and, even, the work and other activities we do with our bodies. In all these areas, we must decide to make sure we glorify God.

Allow me to share one other biblical principle that shows how God's Word applies to every area of one's life. In Hebrews, we find these words.

*Therefore, we also, since we are surrounded by so great a cloud of witnesses, **let us lay aside every weight**, and the sin which so easily ensnares us,* and let us run with endurance the race that is set before us.

Hebrews 12:1

This verse tells Christians it is important to not only lay aside sin but also *every weight* in our lives. That means there are some things that can come into my life that are not actually sin but could weigh me down. When I ran cross country in high school, I could have run a race with combat boots on and carrying a heavy backpack. It wasn't in violation of any rules. However, it would have been foolish to do so because it would have slowed me down, and I wouldn't have had any chance of winning the race. So it is, with our spiritual lives. This picture says it all.

The Principle of Excess

Does it slow me down spiritually?

This principle answers the question, *is there anything in my life weighing me down spiritually?* I cannot allow things in my life that will slow me down in running my spiritual race (God's will) for my life.

We must remember that biblical principles are 100% light and are as important as God's commands in knowing how to live our lives in line with God's purpose and ways. This means God's Word must contain principles that will guide us on how He expects us to educate our children. In the previous chapter, we briefly discussed a few biblical principles found in the definition of Kingdom Education™. In the next chapter, we will look at 14 biblical principles and see how they give Christian parents, church leaders, and educators clear direction on how God wants His people to educate future generations.

Chapter 5

The Importance of Following Directions

"The Bible is an ocean of instruction and wisdom.
Dip daily into the vast pool to discover its truths."[28]
ELIZABETH GEORGE

I HAVE BEEN INVOLVED IN the education of children and youth for more than 50 years. As a teacher, I always stressed to my students the importance of following directions. Some students did not follow my advice, and they consequently suffered some severe consequences they could have avoided if they had only followed the

---

28 George, Elizabeth. n.d. *Quotes.pub.* Accessed 2021. https://www.quotes.
    pub/q/the-bible-is-an-ocean-of-instruction-and-wisdom-dip-daily-in-376295.

directions they were given. To illustrate the importance of following instructions, I want you to look at the following cartoon.

Two little characters go out and lay in the sun. They were both given the same instructions – *put the sunscreen on*! One didn't follow the directions he was given. The result – *burnt to a crisp*! I am going to give each reader an assignment. I am confident that every person reading this will complete this assignment. Even if you are saying to yourself "I am not going to do it no matter what you tell me to do," I believe you will do it. Here is the assignment.

The next time you see a piece of bacon, do not think of this picture!

Of course, when you tell someone not to do something, the natural, almost automatic reaction is to do it. But here is a very serious point I want to make.

The next time you see a piece of bacon and think of this picture, realize that if the home, church, and school do not follow God's directions on how He wants us to educate a child, the false philosophies of this world will burn our children to a crisp!

The sad reality is that most of our children are already suffering from severe sunburns. Our only hope to stop the burn is to *put the sunscreen on,* which is another way of saying *follow God's instructions.*

Remember that Kingdom Education™ only exists when God reigns in the entire process of preparing future generations for life and eternity. He can reign in the education of our children and youth only when His directions are followed.

Even though you won't find a direct reference to the term "education" in the Bible, there are several terms that refer to this important aspect of life. Scripture has much to say about teaching, learning, guiding, instructing, and nurturing. Each of these terms is an action that relates directly to educating future generations.

Over the years of studying God's Word and striving to understand God's plan for educating future generations, I have found several biblical principles that give parents, church leaders, and educators clear directions on *how* God wants His people to educate children and youth. Please note that these principles tell us *how to,* not *where to* educate a child. However, I discovered that when I obeyed God's directions on *how to* educate my children, my options of *where* I could do this became very limited.

In the first edition of *Kingdom Education: God's Plan for Educating Future Generations*, I did not identify any of the biblical principles I had uncovered in my years of searching to understand God's expectations for educating our children. As I shared the message of *Kingdom Education*™, the principles started to crystalize in my mind.

When the second edition was released in 2002, I included eight biblical principles that I had found in Scripture that applied to how Christians were to educate their children. A couple of years later, principles nine and ten were added. For almost 15 years, the number of biblical principles of Kingdom Education™ remained at 10.

Over the past couple of years, God has caused me to study several additional aspects of education from His perspective. Recently, while presenting at our annual Kingdom School Institute, I unveiled four additional principles I believe provide Christians with an even clearer picture of how God wants us to educate future generations.

Words are very important, and it is critical that when using words, we clearly define them. Otherwise, their meanings will be left up to the individual reading them. Several years ago, I was asked to teach a masters-level course at Southwestern Baptist Theological

Seminary. The title of the course was *The Philosophy of Christian School Education*.

Each year, I began the class by asking students what they expected to learn from the title of the course. Their responses included such things as:

- What is a Christian school?
- How does a Christian school operate?
- What is the curriculum of a Christian school?
- What are the basic beliefs and processes involved in Christian schooling?

After this discussion, I informed the class I didn't know how to teach this class. So, I was changing the title to *The Philosophy of Christian Education*. I asked them whether their expectations would change for the course with this new title. Their responses were unanimous. This new title expanded the scope of the education that would be studied. It was broadened from simply Christian schools to all of Christian education. We discussed the differences they expected now that I had changed the course title.

I, then, proceeded to tell them I still didn't know how to teach a course with this title. So, I was changing the title of the course again. Now, the course would be titled *A Christian Philosophy of Education*. The words didn't change, but the order of them did. The class was asked to explain how this new title changed their expectations for the course.

It was agreed that two things changed with this new title for the course. First, the scope of education became even broader than the first two titles. The new course title would cover all of education—not just Christian education.

Second, the scope of the philosophy aspect of the course was narrowed. It was no longer a general philosophy of education class. The course would now present a specific philosophy of education—a Christian philosophy. This would make a huge impact on how these students would look at every educational effort in a child's life.

I then asked a very important question to the students: *What does the term "Christian" mean today?* The responses were immediate and troublesome. The students quickly told me that the term "Christian" has been watered down in its meaning. To many people, the term simply means someone who goes to church once in a while. To others, it meant someone who claims to be "born again." Everyone agreed that the term "Christian" has become very subjective.

At this point, I shared with the class that I was going to change the title of the course one more time. The new and final course title would be *A **Biblical** Philosophy of Education*. By naming the course this way, it removed any subjectivity as to the philosophy of education they were about to study. A "biblical" philosophy of education would base the educational philosophy on an absolute, objective standard—God's Word.

It is vital that Christians know, understand, and commit themselves to a biblical philosophy of education. These 14 biblical principles form the basis for such a philosophy of education. Here are the 14 principles and Scripture references to support them. It is important that parents, church leaders, and educators study each principle and the accompanying Scriptures.

Biblical Principle 1

The education of children and youth is the primary responsibility of parents.
Deuteronomy 6:4-9,11:18-21; Psalms 78;1-7;
Psalms 127:3; Proverbs 22:6;
Malachi 2:13-16; Ephesians 6:4

These passages make it clear that parents are responsible to God for the education or training of their children. Another way of interpreting Psalm 127:3 is *children are God's homework assignment to parents.* Even if parents delegate some areas of their child's education to others, they are still answerable to God for what and how their children are taught.

Malachi 2 makes it clear God desires parents to develop godly offspring. This is an awesome task, and it takes maximum effort on the part of parents to accomplish. As our society becomes more and more secular, we increasingly encounter the false notion that the education of young people is a shared responsibility. Secularists say parents do have certain responsibilities but so do the local, state, and federal governments. At each level of government, various branches are constantly vying to assume more and more of this responsibility. However, in the end, God will hold parents accountable for how they educated their children.

Biblical Principle 2

> *The education of children and youth is a 24-hour-a-day,*
> *seven-days-per-week process that continues from birth till*
> *maturity.*
>
> Deuteronomy 6:7, 11:19; Proverbs 22:6

A high percentage of Christian parents have heard and even memorized Proverbs 22:6. We want to claim this as a promise that will assure us that our children will eventually walk with the Lord if we give them some training from a biblical perspective early in life. However, most of us fail to comprehend how intense this training needs to be.

The concept communicated by the phrase *train up a child* is that this is a continuous process that starts at birth. *When he is old* tells us that this process does not end until the individual reaches maturity.

God gives us instruction in Deuteronomy 6 when He states that parents must teach their children diligently with intense, highly concentrated, consistent effort. This effort must take place:

1. When our children get up each morning
2. When they are at home and around the house
3. When they are away from the house, and
4. When they lie down to go to sleep.

The only time we should not be diligently teaching our children the things of God is when they are asleep. Since the education of children and youth is a 24/7 process, it requires that the home, church, and school partner together to ensure every child receives a biblical worldview education.

Biblical Principle 3

> *The education of children and youth must have as its*
> *primary goals the salvation of and discipleship of the next*
> *generation.*
>
> Psalms 78:6-7; Matthew 28:19-20

Philip May, in his book *Which Way to Educate,* compares today's educator to the field general who has become so involved in the details and strategies of the immediate battle that he has lost sight of the overall strategy of the war or has actually forgotten why it is being fought.[29] Christians must never forget that the only goal with true meaning for why we educate our children is for them to know Jesus Christ as their personal Savior.

If our children become National Merit Scholars and do not know Christ, what have we achieved of lasting value? Christ told His disciples He wanted them to make other disciples, giving them a new identity in Christ and empowering them into a lifelong relationship with Christ characterized by love, trust, and obedience.

As we assume our responsibilities to diligently teach our children God's ways, and we do this all day long, we must also strive to see them follow Christ in all they do. In fact, we can know that we have been successful in this task when we see our children and our grandchildren teach their children to know God and keep His commandments (Psalm 78:6-7).

---

29   Philip May, *Which Way to Educate.* (Chicago: Moody Press, 1975), 9

Biblical Principle 4

The education of children and youth must be based on God's Word as absolute truth.

Matthew 24:35; Psalms 119

Man constantly searches for truth. Life has no meaning apart from truth. When Pilate was trying to make sense out of the dilemma he faced concerning Jesus, he asked Jesus, *"What is truth?"* (John 18:38, KJV). Our society declares truth is determined only by experience. It has been redefined as anything that is *"legally accurate."* But God's Word is eternal and, therefore, is man's only source of truth. This means that everything man studies must be scrutinized through the lens of Scripture, the only way to find true knowledge that will lead us to wisdom.

When God's Word is removed from any facet of education, that education becomes mere human indoctrination. Such education always evolves into empty philosophies that spoil and deceive children because it follows after the traditions of man and the rudiments of the world rather than after Christ. Whatever is taught to our children and youth must be based on the absolute truth found in God's Word. This is true for wherever education takes place—at home, in the church, or at school.

Biblical Principle 5

> *The education of children and youth must hold Christ as preeminent in all of life.*
>
> Colossians 2:3, 6-10

Because of the sacrifice Christ made on the cross on behalf of all men and in humble obedience to His Father, His name has been exalted above all other names. In fact, the Bible states that Jesus not only created everything but everything was created for Him.

Christ is to be preeminent in everything – period. The education of children and youth must be centered on Christ. By doing this, it will lead us to the goal of seeing our children living in a personal, intimate love relationship with Jesus. Christ must be at the center or heart of all that is taught to our children. In the 1600s, John Milton wrote, *"the end then of learning is to repair the ruins of our first parents by regaining to know God aright, and out of that knowledge to love Him, to imitate Him, to be like Him."*[30]

Biblical Principle 6

> *The education of children and youth must not hinder the spiritual and moral development of the next generation.*
>
> Matthew 18:6; 19:13-14;
> Mark 10:13-16; Luke 18:15-17

---

30   John Milton, "Of Education," in *Basic Writings in Christian Education,* ed. Kendig Brubaker Cully. (Philadelphia: Westminster Press, 1960) 24.

Jesus showed a special love for children throughout His earthly ministry. When the disciples tried to keep children from getting too close to Jesus, He rebuked them very firmly. It was in this context that Jesus made statements about the seriousness of offending a young person, as noted in the passages above.

Sometimes, we think of offending children only by means of physical abuse, but anything that hinders their moral and spiritual development is the epitome of child abuse. It is vitally important that the education a child receives at home, church, and/or school draws them closer to Jesus and does not hinder their spiritual formation.

Biblical Principle 7

> *The education of children and youth, if and when delegated to others by parents, must be done so with utmost care to ensure that all teachers follow these principles.*
> Exodus 18:21; I Samuel 1:27-28, 3:1-10

The task of raising children is awesome. It is becoming more demanding with each passing day. Every parent will in some way delegate some of the responsibility in the process of properly educating their children. This happens when we take them to church, allow them to go on the Internet, or send them to school.

When Moses was trying to educate the children of Israel to know and follow God, Jethro told him he had better delegate some of the tasks to others if he planned to survive. However, Jethro warned Moses to be extremely careful to check the character of the person to whom he would delegate any portion of this responsibility. In essence, each person had to fear God, love truth, and hate covetousness (Exodus 18:21). Parents must carefully choose to whom they will delegate some of their responsibility of educating their children. These people must follow the biblical principles of Kingdom Education™.

Biblical Principle 8

The education of children and youth results in the formation of a belief system or worldview that will be patterned after the belief systems or worldviews of the person's teachers.

Luke 6:40

Every person has a worldview or an underlying belief system that drives his or her attitudes and actions in life. A person can hold one of two possible worldviews: a God-centered worldview or a man-centered worldview. The individual's worldview is primarily determined by that of his teachers.

Everyone who teaches others influences them in three ways: by his or her content (or what they say), by his or her communication (or how they say it), and by his or her conduct (or how they live). No one can teach out of a philosophical vacuum. Their beliefs and values will be communicated to the students, and their worldview will help shape the beliefs and values of those they teach.

George Barna claims that only 7-8% of today's Christians have a biblical understanding of life. Following this principle would cause us to conclude that today's Christians have been educated by a majority of people (influences) who did not possess a God-centered worldview.

Biblical Principle 9

The education of children and youth must lead to true wisdom by connecting all knowledge to a biblical worldview for frame of reference.
Romans 1:20; Psalm 19:1; Proverbs 4:5, 7, 3:19, 9:10, Psalms 104:24; 136:5; Jeremiah 10:12; Romans 11:33; Luke 11:52; Colossians 2:3; 1 Corinthians 8:1; 13:8; Romans 1:28

Nancy Pearcy in her book *Total Truth* states, *"We must begin by being utterly convinced that there is a biblical perspective on everything—not just on spiritual matters....The fear of some 'god' is the beginning of every proposed system of knowledge....God is the sole source of the entire created order. No other gods compete with Him; no forces exist on their own; nothing receives its nature or existence from another source. Thus, His Word, or laws or creation ordinances, give the world its order and structure....There is no philosophically or spiritually neutral subject."*[31]

God created the entire universe—including every fact found in every subject one studies. Scripture makes it clear God reveals His very character and nature to us through our understanding of His created world (Romans 1:20). The education that we provide our children must not merely give our children knowledge but must lead to true

---

31   Nancy Pearcey, *Total Truth: Liberating Christianity from Its Cultural Captivity.* (Wheaton, IL: Crossway Books), 44, 45.

wisdom and understanding by causing children to see the God-intended meaning found in everything they study.

If any part of our children's education is presented as spiritually neutral, our children may think God is irrelevant to some aspects of life. This will lead them to divide their lives into two compartments—the secular and the sacred.

Biblical Principle 10

The education of children and youth must have a view of the future that includes the eternal perspective.
Colossians 3:1-2; Matthew 6:19-20;
2 Timothy 4:6-8; Acts 20:24;
Hebrews 11:13; Colossians 3:23-24

God places a two-fold calling on every child's life. The first and most important call on a child's life is an eternal call. God desires each child to come to know Jesus Christ as his or her personal Lord and Savior. The second call is a temporal call. This involves God's call for a person to live a life of service to Christ while here on earth.

The education of children and youth must not only prepare them for a life of service here but also to stand before God for eternity. This eternal perspective must be part of the entire educational process. It is very natural to focus only on this temporal life when it comes to education. But if this is the only focus of education, then individual success will be measured in temporal financial achievement. Financial success is the dominant goal of secular education today. The home, church, and school must understand that the education of our children and youth must prepare them for life and eternity.

Biblical Principle 11

> *The education of children and youth must have as its primary focus an increase in knowledge of God.*
>
> John 17:3; Romans 1:20; Romans 11:33-36;
> Psalm 19:1-6; Ephesians 1:16-19, 3:15-19, 4:13;
> Philippians 1:9; 3:8-10, 13-14;
> Colossians 1:9-10, 2:2-3; 2 Peter 3:18;
> Proverbs 2:5; Hosea 4:1, 6:6; 2 Corinthians 10:3-5

All education involves gaining knowledge. This is true whether the education takes place in the home, church, or school. Unfortunately, not all knowledge is of equal importance or value. Knowledge is exploding at exponential rates all around the world. Because of the internet, our children and youth are constantly being bombarded with knowledge that really has no direct impact on their lives. In his book, *Handoff: The Only Way to Win the Race of Life*, Dr. Jeff Myers says this about all the information bombarding us today:

> *Information overload breaks down a person's capacity for discernment...It presents so much information that we find it impossible to figure out what is truly important.*[32]

Schooling emphasizes the importance of students gaining knowledge by stressing the need for them to excel on a wide variety of tests and

---

32 Jeff Myers, *Handoff.* (Legacy Worldwide Publishers, 2008).

examinations. SAT and ACT scores, honors and AP course grades, and a host of other academic efforts are held in high esteem. But parents, church leaders, and educators must understand what God's Word says about the importance of gaining knowledge. The book of Proverbs stresses the importance of gaining knowledge; however, it goes on to say that when attaining knowledge, it is also important to obtain wisdom and understanding. The reason students need to obtain wisdom and understanding is that God expects His people to use the knowledge they obtain to advance His Kingdom. Merely learning facts in order to achieve higher test scores and get accepted into college is not what God wants from His people.

Therefore, it is critical that Christians keep the major focus of education on increasing students' knowledge of God. God created man in His image so that man could know Him. Man was created for relationship. J.I. Packer states, *Once you become aware that the main business you are here for is to know God, most of life's problems fall in place of their own accord.*[33] As one studies the Scriptures above, they will understand the priority of making sure the education children and youth receive focuses on the increase in knowledge of God.

Biblical Principle 12

The education of children and youth results in performing work in fulfillment of God's will for their lives.
Genesis 1:26; Matthew 6:10, 33;
Ephesians 5:17; Hebrews 10:36, 13:20-21;
Colossians 1:9-10, 12:1-2; Proverbs 3:5-6, 20:24

33   J. I. Packer, *Knowing God.* (Downers Grover, IL: InterVarsity Press, 1973), 29.

Most Christian parents would say they want their children to grow up and find God's will for their lives. However, few parents understand that finding God's will for their lives should be the main result of the education they receive. This, again, must be true for the education children and youth receive at home, church, and school.

As stated previously, God places two calls on everyone's life. This principal addresses God's second call. That call is a specific call to do work for His glory. Man was created to work because man was created in the image of God, one who is constantly at work in His creation.

Every child has been given specific gifts and abilities by God in order for him or her to engage with some aspect of God's creation. Every person's calling or purpose is to be a steward of some aspect of creation. Consider the words of Kevin Swanson in his book, *Upgrade*:

> *Everybody is gifted and has a purpose in God's world.... Each child has a specific calling, framed by his unique talents and abilities....A successful education is achieved when a child is prepared to make maximal use of his God-given talents and abilities in the accomplishment of the child's calling....The challenge of the first eighteen years of a child's education is to find that calling....A fulfilled life will be determined by whether he/she has centered in upon his or her life calling.*[34]

---

34   Swanson, 13-19.

Biblical Principle 13

The education of children and youth must be characterized by the pursuit of biblical excellence based on godly character, resulting in competent performance.
2 Corinthians 8:7, 10:12; Philippians 1:9-10, 4:8;
1 Timothy 6:11; Psalm 8:1; Ecclesiastes 9:10

The pursuit of excellence should be a key aspect of the education every child receives at home, church, or school. This is because God's name, alone, is excellent. As you consider this principle, take a minute and write down your definition of excellence. Most Christians, when asked to do this, will define excellence based on one's performance and/or achievement. Unfortunately, the majority of Christians have adopted a worldly picture of excellence.

The world sees excellence from only a horizontal perspective. It can be summed up by two words – *compare* and *compete*. An individual or an organization/team/etc. is "excellent" if it is better than the others. In a postmodern, post-truth world, excellence is subjective in nature. Achievement and performance become the measure of success.

The Apostle Paul warned Christians in Corinth about the danger of measuring oneself through comparison with other people (see 2 Corinthians 10:12). Christians must pursue biblically-based excellence. This excellence begins with a vertical perspective. Biblical excellence has several characteristics that are in stark contrast with the world's idea of excellence. True excellence has the following characteristics.

- God is the standard for excellence.
- Jesus is the model of excellence.
- Christlikeness is the goal of excellence.
- Character, not performance, is the primary focus of excellence.
- God's glory is the motive for excellence.
- The Bible, not human opinion, provides characteristics of excellence.
- God's spirit is the empowerment to achieve excellence.

Performance and/or achievement are important to pursuing biblically-based excellence. However, performance/achievement only has eternal significance if it is an extension of striving for Godly character in one's life. A person should strive to do their best in every endeavor because they represent Jesus Christ. When this is accomplished, a student not only achieves excellence but is a success in God's eyes.

Biblical Principle 14

> *The education of children and youth must equip them to fulfill God's highest purpose for man: to glorify Him and enjoy Him in life and eternity.*
>   Romans 11:36; Colossians 1:16-17; Genesis 1:26-27;
>   Isaiah 42:8; Psalms 19:1-3; Romans 1:20;
>   Hebrews 1:3; 1 Corinthians 6:19-20, 10:31

The Westminster Shorter Catechism begins by asking a very important question: *What is the chief end for man?* The answer to the question gives every Christian an understanding of God's highest purpose for every child born into this world. In the catechism, the following answer is given: *Man's chief end is to glorify God and to enjoy Him forever.*

When one studies the Scriptures listed above, he or she finds that God created the heavens and the earth as an expression of who He is (see Romans 1:20 and Psalm 19:1-3). He created everything, including man, for Himself (see Romans 11:36 and Colossians 1:16-17). In other words, everything was created for His glory, which means that the education a child receives should prepare him or her to fulfill God's highest purpose for his or her life – to give Him glory through everything they think, say, and do.

All Christian parents want God to bless their children and give them success in life. As one considers Isaiah 42:8, he or she find that God will only work for His glory. Therefore, education must equip a student to be able to live a life that glorifies God. It is important to understand, in a practical way, what it means to glorify God. Dr. Gary Inrig said it best when he wrote.

> *One's glory is one's reputation....God's glory is not just His reputation but His revealed character, the display of His attributes. To glorify someone, therefore, is to increase his reputation by revealing his true nature....to glorify God is to live in such a way that **His character is displayed and His praise is increased**.*[35]

God's purpose for education is that every young person is so trained and equipped that his or her life displays God's character and God's praise is increased.

---

35   Gary Inrig, *A Call to Excellence*. (Victor Books: Wheaton IL, 1985), 56.

Chapter 6

Obedience Not Optional

"Sow a thought, and you reap an act;
Sow and act, and you reap a habit;
Sow a habit and you reap a character;
Sow a character, and you reap a destiny."[36]
CHARLES READE

THERE ARE SOME LAWS OR ORDINANCES or principles everyone must obey. It doesn't matter how obstinate or rebellious a person might be, he or she will obey certain rules. For example, everyone obeys the law of gravity. You can stand on a rooftop and defiantly say that you will not obey this law. But if you step off the roof, you will fall to the ground.

---

36 Reade, Charles. n.d. *Quotetab: Charles Reade Quotations.* Accessed 2021. https://www.quotetab.com/quotes/by-charles-reade.

There are two such principles that I have become convicted about over the past year or so. These two life principles impact the education we give our children and youth. Individuals, parents, church leaders, and teachers will obey them as they teach future generations.

Life Principle 1

The first principle I want us to look at was set in place at the very beginning of time. In a Breakpoint article, Eric Metaxas explained that *when God created the world, He set up a series of observable, rational laws to govern it.*[37] Nancy Pearcey refers to these laws as *creation ordinances.* When God spoke this world into existence, this life principle was the very first creation ordinance He set in place. You will find this life principle introduced in Genesis 1 and then explained and emphasized throughout Scripture. Consider these verses.

> *Then God said, "Let the earth bring forth grass, the herb that yields seed, and the fruit tree that yields fruit according to its kind, whose seed is in itself, on the earth"; and it was so. And the earth brought forth grass, the herb that yields seed according to its kind, and the tree that yields fruit, whose seed is in itself according to its kind.*
>
> Genesis 1:11-12

> *Then God said, "Let the waters abound with an abundance of living creatures, and let birds fly above the earth across the face of the firmament of the heavens." So God created*

---

37 Eric Metaxas, "BreakPoint: Scientists and Christianity," https://breakpoint.org/, January 23, 2018.

great sea creatures and every living thing that moves, with which the waters abounded, according to their kind, and every winged bird according to its kind.

Genesis 1:20-21

Then God said, "Let the earth bring forth the living creature according to its kind: cattle and creeping thing and beast of the earth, each according to its kind"; and it was so. And God made the beast of the earth according to its kind, cattle according to its kind, and everything that creeps on the earth according to its kind.

Genesis 1:24-25

Did you see it? As you read these verses, did you catch this life principle—God's first creation ordinance? Every time God created some form of life, He put this ordinance into operation. It is found in these words—*according to its kind.* This first life principle can be stated this way.

What one plants, one harvests!

This principle is often referred to as the law of the harvest. Whatever one sows, he will reap. It must be noted that obedience isn't optional. This principle cannot be negated. You can plant a kernel of corn and, try your best, you will not grow a cherry tree. It is impossible! All of created life reproduces only after its kind. This is why evolution is an impossibility. Lower life forms cannot produce higher life forms. It is contrary to God's first creation ordinance.

This principle also holds true in our everyday lives. God's Word tells us that if we want to be given mercy, we must plant mercy in other people's lives. If we give, it will be given back to us. God even tells us that if we ignore Him, He will ignore our children (see Hosea 4:6b). Paul summed this up in his letter to the Galatian Christians:

> *Do not be deceived, God is not mocked; for whatever a man sows, that he will also reap. For he who sows to his flesh will of the flesh reap corruption, but he who sows to the Spirit will of the Spirit reap everlasting life.*
>
> Galatians 6:7-8

Life Principle 2

The second life principle that we must understand can be explained this way: If I were to call each of my three children on the phone and tell them I am going to give each of them $10,000 for Christmas, their response would be one of laughter. I can hear them say, *Sure, dad, now what will you really give us?* Even if I try to convince them that I am really going to do this, they won't believe it. Why? It is because of the simple fact that they know I don't have $30,000 to my name.

This, life principle 2 can be stated this way:

You can only give what you possess!

Again, this principle must be obeyed. Jesus noted how the widow who gave her two mites gave all that she possessed. When Elijah asked another widow to make him some bread to eat, she explained that she just had enough to make some bread for her and her son. This is all she had, and after it was gone, they would die. She could not give to Elijah and also to her son. She could only give what she possessed.

Both of these life principles have major implications on the education we provide our children and youth. We will see how they impact our children's education in the next two chapters. For now, I want us to recognize and understand them and how they are in operation in every area of our lives. Remember, when it comes to these two life principles, obedience is not optional! Even if one doesn't obey them, they will eventually reap the consequences of their decisions.

Chapter 7

Freedom from Captivity

"We accept the truth or reject it,
but we can't ignore it!"[38]
FRANK TUREK

THERE IS A VERSE IN THE BIBLE that has had a grip on me for most of my time in ministry. It is found in Paul's letter to the Colossian Christians. Most Christians are familiar with it, and many may have even memorized it. However, far too few Christians understand the disastrous implications this verse has if it isn't heeded. The verse reads:

---

38   Frank Turek, Twitter post, April 24, 2019, https://twitter.com/drfrankturek.

> *Beware lest anyone cheat you through philosophy and empty deceit, according to the tradition of men, according to the basic principles of the world, and not according to Christ.*
>
> Colossians 2:8

The word "cheat" is translated as "spoil" or "captive" in other translations. In the original language, it means "seduced" or "led away as booty." Paul is warning Christians not to be taken captive by false philosophy or the basic beliefs/values of the world. We can substitute the term "worldview" or "ideas" for the word "philosophy" in this verse. Paul is telling us to be alert and not be taken captive by false ideas.

Since Paul is writing to Christians, it means Christians are in danger of being taken captive by false ideas or worldviews. If Christians were immune to this, Paul wouldn't have needed to warn us. The reality is that all adult Christians have been taken captive by some ideas or worldview. Unfortunately, too many Christians have allowed themselves to be taken captive by a false belief system/worldview.

This verse also helps us identify false philosophies or worldviews. False ideas always follow the tradition of men and/or the basic principles of the world. If you want to know what the basic principles of the world are, simply look at today's culture. It reflects the principles of the world – not Christ.

We must also remember that Jesus Christ is the Word (John 1). Therefore, the verse can be paraphrased to read,

> *Be on guard and don't let anyone take you captive through false ideas or worldviews that follow the tradition of men*

*and the basic ways of the culture and not in line with
the Word.*

My former pastor, Dr. Michael Catt, was preaching a sermon once
and made a profound statement. He didn't make the statement about
this verse. However, as soon as he said it, my mind went straight to
Colossians 2:8. He said,

It is easier to be traditional than it is to be biblical!

It is easy to follow the tradition of men when it comes to educating our
children and youth. It is even quite easy to operate a traditional Christian
school. However, it is far more difficult to educate our children biblically
and/or operate a biblical Christian school.

Two facts must be grasped about being taken captive by false ideas. The
first fact is that being taken captive by ideas is extremely subtle. You
don't even know it is taking place.

Here is a simple question that I often ask parents: Has there been a time
when one of your children has done a very dumb thing? Whenever I
ask that question, laughter goes through the audience. You can hear
some quietly say things like, "Just one of my children?" or "Or just one
time?" The truth of the matter is that every parent knows of multiple
times their children do really dumb things.

I usually follow that up with another question: When you witness
your child doing something dumb, is your question to them this?
"What were you _____?" I will pause without finishing the
question, but immediately, everyone finishes the question for me by

saying "thinking." We ask them what they were thinking because we know that they didn't just wake up and decide to do something dumb. They had to first think about doing it.

When you ask a child, "What were you thinking?" what is the common response from the child? Again, everyone quickly responds, "I don't know." This is followed by laughter. A child's answer of "I don't know" is a very honest one. They don't know what they were thinking. Why? Because they weren't aware that they had been taken captive by some very bad ideas.

The second fact about being taken captive by false ideas is that one gets more than they wanted or imagined. We often think that we can dabble in the world of false ideas. We say to ourselves, *we are Christians, and we can handle it.* However, truth be known, we can't handle it. And once a false worldview takes you or me captive, the consequences go far beyond what we dreamed possible.

Kevin Swanson puts it this way in his book, *Upgrade*:

> *If wrong ideas are communicated to your children, it will certainly have an effect on how they live. If the wrong ideas are communicated to a great many children through education, that could very well undermine our entire civilization.*[39]

For decades, Christians have turned their children over to the world to educate them. The result is that we are losing generation after generation

---

39   Swanson, 162-163.

of young people to the world. How would you respond to the following question?

Does the rioting, looting, and destruction of private property we are seeing take place before our very eyes bother you? We shouldn't be shocked. It is evidence that younger generations have been taken captive by false ideas. These false ideas carry with them severe consequences. How bad is it? Is it true what author Harry Blamires wrote in 1963?

> *There is no longer a Christian mind...the modern Christian has succumbed to secularization.*[40]

Most parents, church leaders, and educators have not realized the extent that Colossians 2:8 is a reality in the hearts and minds of the next generation. Maybe the reason they haven't grasped this is that we, too, have been taken captive by a false worldview. In the next chapter, we will examine the worldview crisis that is plaguing today's church.

---

40   Harry Blamires, *The Christian Mind.* (Ann Arbor, MI: Servant Books, 1963), 3.

Chapter 8

A Worldview Crisis

"...We are in a white-hot battle for the
hearts and minds of young people.
Leftist radicals know it, Richard Dawkins and
the New Atheists know it, and we, as Christians,
of all people, had better know it."[41]
DR. ALBERT MOHLER

ONE OF THE MOST IMPORTANT ASPECTS of the education we give to future generations is the impact an individual's or group's worldview has on the hearts and minds of children and youth. One's worldview, whether it is a parent, pastor, teacher, coach, author,

---

41 Albert Mohler, "The Briefing: Monday, October 7, 2019," Albert Mohler, October 7, 2019, https://albertmohler.com/2019/10/07/briefing-10-7-19.

etc., is a major influence on the development of future generations' worldviews or belief systems.

At the center of every educational effort lies someone's worldview trying to capture the mind and heart of the student. John Stonestreet and Brett Kunkle emphasize this truth in their book, *A Guide to Culture*. In this book, the authors make this point:

> *Every song, movie, Tweet, sermon, news story, podcast, banner ad, and billboard tells us something about what to believe and how to live....the information we think is inconsequential to our lives still communicates ideas about life and the world.*[42]

They go on to state that ideas or worldviews are trying to influence the way we think and live:

> *If ideas stayed safely in their books...then batting them around would be...harmless. But they don't stay in books. They grow legs, walk off the pages, and influence the way we think and live.*[43]

We must never forget that the main business of all education is the communication of ideas or worldviews, and all ideas have consequences. In fact, Stonestreet and Kunkle make the point that *bad ideas have victims.*

---

42   John Stonestreet and Brett Kunkle, *A Practical Guide to Culture*. (Colorado Springs, CO: David C. Cook, 2017), 79.

43   Stonestreet and Kunkle, 80.

Unfortunately, there is a major worldview crisis in today's church. Dr. George Barna is the director of research at the Cultural Research Center at Arizona Christian University. Over the past few years, Dr. Barna has been conducting major research on the worldviews held by Christians. The findings were published in the *American Worldview Inventory 2020*. Some of the findings are presented in the table below.

Examples of Christians' Beliefs That Differ from Biblical Teaching[44]				
	% that *reject* this biblical teaching			
Biblical teaching	Evang.	Pent.	Main	Catholic
People are not basically good; we are sinners.	75%	76%	81%	84%
There are absolute moral truths that apply to everyone all the time.	52%	69%	58%	69%
People cannot earn a place in Heaven by being good or by doing good works.	58%	49%	61%	85%
The Bible is the primary source of moral guidance.	42%	38%	71%	77%
Bible is the Word of God and is trustworthy and reliable.	26%	32%	63%	53%
Human life is sacred.	40%	54%	55%	57%

These findings indicate that a majority of self-identified Christians actually **reject** many truths found in Scripture. It must be noted that one's beliefs are based on one's worldview. These results indicate that a large number of Christians do not possess a biblical worldview.

---

44   Arizona Christian University. 2021. *Cultural Research Center*. Accessed 2021. https://www.arizonachristian.edu/culturalresearchcenter/research/.

At a worldview conference I was speaking at recently, Dr. Barna reported his findings on a study that showed how many adults possess a biblical worldview. This study broke adults down by the various generations alive today. A summary of his presentation is presented below:[45]

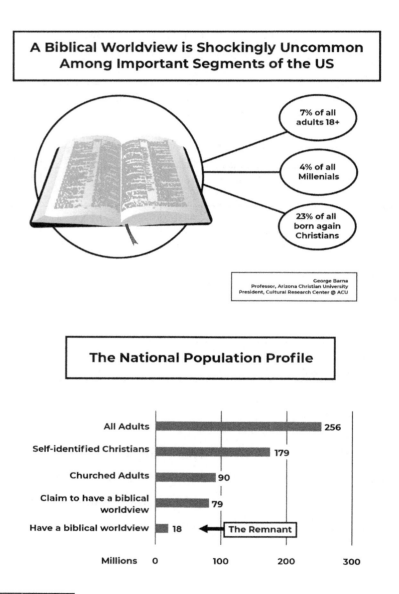

45   VIP Worldview Conference, Museum of the Bible, March 30-April 1, 2021

These two charts clearly show there is a worldview crisis in today's church. This crisis is having a major impact on younger generations. I just finished reading another report recently released by the PINETOPS Foundation entitled *The Great Opportunity: The American Church in 2050.* This study makes some stark predictions about what will happen over the next 30 years if something doesn't change. Below, I highlight some of the findings that I found most startling:

Thirty-five million youths raised in Christian families are projected to disaffiliate from Christianity by the year 2050. It may be worse, where as many as 42 million people raised in Christian homes may no longer say they are Christians.

Christianity in America will make up just 59% of the country's population by 2050, compared to 73% today.

It will be the largest and fastest numerical shift in religious affiliation in the history of the country.[46]

Why are we seeing findings like the ones above? It is because, for decades, the vast majority of Christians have provided their children and youth with a secular worldview education. This is true for the vast majority of Christian homes, churches, and schools.

The current demise of today's culture, due to decades of secular education, was predicted to take place more than 100 years ago. Dr. Robert Lewis Dabney was a professor of moral philosophy at the University of Texas in

---

46   Pinetops Foundation. 2020. *The Great Opportunity.* Accessed 2021. https:// www.greatopportunity.org/.

the late 1800s. Dabney made some major predictions about what would happen if the education of children and youth became the responsibility of the government. In one of his writings, *Volume IV: Secular*, Dabney gave these warnings:

> *If the state in America becomes the educator, education must be secularized completely....there is therefore a great risk that the education of youth will be perverted to serve an ideological faction. This will occur by the hateful means of filling their minds with error and passion in place of truth and right.*[47]

Dabney went on to warn Christians to be prepared for what he foresaw to be the inevitable result if this were to happen.

> *But nearly all public men and preachers declare that the public schools are the glory of America. They are a finality and in no event to be surrendered.* **And we have seen that their complete secularization is logically inevitable. Christians must prepare themselves, then, for the following results: All prayers, catechisms, and Bibles will ultimately be driven out of the schools.**[48]

Daniel Webster was another person who warned about the danger of excluding Christianity from college.

---

47   Robert L Dabney, *Discussions, Volume IV Secular*, Crescent Book House, Mexico, MO 1897   http://www.thecontinuingwitness.com/uploads/9/8/2/3/98238342/rld_secularized_education.pdf

48   Dabney

In what age, by what sect, where, when, by whom, has religious truth been excluded from education? Nowhere. Never! Everywhere, and at all times, it has been regarded as essential. **It is of the essence, the vitality of useful instruction.**[49]

In the early to mid-1900s, Dr. Charles Francis Potter became a very strong voice in the education world of the day. Potter was one of the original 34 signers of the *Humanist Manifesto.* He was the founder of the First Humanist Society of NY. Its stated philosophy is summed up in these words.

Faith in the supreme value and self-perfectibility of human personality, conceived socially as well as individually.[50]

Potter was convinced that humanistic, secular education would eventually control the hearts and minds of future generations. In his book, *Humanism: A New Religion*, Potter stated this conviction with these words:

Education is thus a most powerful ally of humanism, and every American public school is a school of humanism. What can the theistic Sunday schools, meeting for an hour once a week, teaching only a fraction of the children, do to stem the tide of a five-day program of humanistic teaching?[51]

---

49 Daniel Webster, quoted in Dabney.

50 Stringer-Hye, Richard. 2001. *Charles Francis Potter.* May 17. Accessed 2021. https://uudb.org/articles/charlesfrancispotter.html.

51 Charles Francis Potter, *Humanism: A New Religion.* (New York, NY: Simon and Schuster 1930), 128.

What these men and many others predicted has all become true, which has resulted in the majority of Christians developing a secular worldview that is driving all their actions and attitudes in life.

Barna explains the crisis we are facing in the church today by sharing some facts we must get our minds to comprehend. It is now believed that a person's basic worldview is shaped by the age of 13. One's worldview will be refined and adjusted between the ages of 14 and 30, but his/her basic beliefs about life will not change.

This means that the primary parenting generation for this age group is the Millennial generation. This generation is also fast becoming the primary teaching generation in churches and schools. Studies indicate that only 4%, one out of 25, of Millennials have a biblical worldview. In fact, a more recent study suggests that the percentage of Millennials that have a biblical worldview may be as low as 2%.

Consider the words of Dr. Tony Evans:

> *Children have a very spiritual reason for their existence…*
> *[parents] are to transfer a theocentric, God-centered*
> *worldview; that's why He said to raise them in the Lord.*
> *Let the glasses they wear, we call that a worldview, a lens*
> *through which you view life, be constructed by the parents*
> *as they have gotten it from the Lord.*[52]

---

52   Tony Evans, "Raising Kingdom Kids" (The Kingdom Family sermon series, Oakcliff Bible Church, Dallas Texas) .

Kingdom Education™ holds to the biblical truth that parents are the ones God has given the primary responsibility to educate their children biblically. This is exactly what Evans is saying. He makes it clear that biblical education requires parents to help their children develop a biblical worldview. The church and school must partner with the home in helping parents accomplish this task. Evans goes on to state,

> But if the parents haven't gotten anything, they can't give anything.
> We are to transfer to them [children] what we have gotten from the Lord.[53]

Here, we find the two life principles presented in the Chapter 6 being played out before our very eyes. The current adult generations, for the most part, do not possess a biblical worldview. One can only give what one possesses. This means that it is next to impossible for the next generation of young people to develop a biblical worldview. Why? Because those who will be teaching them at home, church, and school most likely do not possess a biblical worldview themselves. Therefore, they cannot give what they, themselves, don't have.

At the same time, the first life principle will be played out. Since the majority of Christian adults do not have a biblical worldview, it means that they have a secular one. At best, Christians may have a dualistic worldview, but that means that biblical truth will only be applied to the "spiritual" compartment of life.

---

53   Tony Evans, "Raising Kingdom Kids."

In either case, parents, church leaders, and educators can only plant their worldview in the hearts and minds of the next generation. According to God's first creation ordinance, such planting will only result in future generations living their lives from a secular worldview perspective.

Something must change. But what must happen, and how can it take place?

C h a p t e r   9

A Call to Action!

"God's primary goal for your life is not your happiness
but His glory. Don't be surprised when
He leads your life with that end!
Learn to be happy when He is glorified!"[54]
RICHARD BLACKABY

TODAY'S WORLDVIEW CRISIS REQUIRES immediate action on the part of all Christians. But what action must take place? As with all spiritual issues, it must start with us as individuals. If I don't change, my home won't change, nor will my church or school.

The first thing we, as individuals, must do is repent for not addressing the issue of education biblically for the past several decades. We must

---

54 Richard Blackaby, Twitter post, June 10, 2019, 6:12 a.m., https://twitter.com/
    richardblackaby/status/1138041189112958977.

seek God's forgiveness for not following His directions on how He expects us to educate children and youth.

The next step in reversing the current trends is to follow Paul's admonition to the church in Rome:

> *Do not be conformed to this world,*
> *but be transformed by the renewing of your mind.*
>
> Romans 12:2

We will never see our children develop a biblical worldview and become strong disciples of Jesus Christ if we don't change our stinkin' thinkin'! We must understand that we have been taken captive by false ideas, as Paul explained can happen in Colossians 2:8. We must realize that when one attempts to renew one's mind, that person is entering into fierce spiritual warfare. Again, we need to look at how Paul describes this war in his second letter to the church at Corinth:

> *For though we walk in the flesh, we do not war according*
> *to the flesh. For the weapons of our warfare are not carnal*
> *but mighty in God for pulling down strongholds, casting*
> *down arguments and every high thing that exalts itself*
> *against the knowledge of God, bringing every thought into*
> *captivity to the obedience of Christ, and being ready to*
> *punish all disobedience when our obedience is fulfilled.*
>
> 2 Corinthians 1:3-6

Renewing one's mind is definitely a spiritual battle. It is a battle for the mind. The reason this is such an intense battle is that our minds control our lives (see Proverbs 23:7). A person does not develop his/her worldview in just a matter of minutes. It takes a lifetime for our belief system to be fully formed.

When we recognize that we have a false worldview and need to change it, it will take all of our energy to do so. Be prepared for a lengthy fight. This won't happen overnight. In fact, we will always be engaged in the battle to renew our minds as long as we are alive in this fallen world.

I encourage you to read Nehemiah 13:4-9. I believe this passage of Scripture provides us with another picture of what it takes to renew the mind. I explain this passage in detail in my chapter on renewing the mind in my book, *Kingdom Education*.

God's Word tells us how we can be set free from being taken captive by false ideas. To understand this, there are a couple of passages in God's Word that we must look at. The first is found in the book of John. This very familiar verse reads,

> *Jesus said to him "I am the way, the truth, and the life; no one comes to the Father except through Me."*
>
> John 14:6

Here, we find Jesus declaring that ***He is truth!*** Truth is not something God decided while sitting up in Heaven. No, truth is a person. It is who God is! The prophet Isaiah said this about Jesus:

> *He has sent Me to heal the brokenhearted, to proclaim liberty to the captives, and the opening of the prison to those who are bound.*
>
> Isaiah 61:1

I know that this verse applies to the captivity all mankind is under due to sin. However, I also believe that it is saying Jesus is the key to being set free from the captivity of false ideas or worldviews. This is seen when Jesus was talking to some new believers.

> *Then Jesus said to those Jews who believed Him, "If you abide in My word, you are My disciples indeed. And you shall know the truth, and the truth shall set you free."*
>
> John 8:31-32

Too many Christians merely memorize the last part of this passage— when one knows the truth, they will be free. But we have to understand the full lesson Jesus was teaching in this passage.

Jesus identifies three groups of people in this passage. The first group is made up of people who are "believers." He was talking to "those Jews who believed Him." The second group is assumed. They are the "unbelievers." If some Jews believed Him, it implies that there were some who didn't. The third and final group were the "disciples."

Jesus told those who were "believers" that if they abide in His Word, they would, then, become "disciples." To "abide" means to dwell or live in. There is a difference between visiting someone's home and actually living or dwelling there. Jesus is saying, "if you want to be my disciple, you can't merely visit My Word once in a while. You must dwell in it."

Jesus explained that once you do this ("dwell in My Word") and become His disciple, then you, as a disciple, will know the truth and be set free. Freedom from the captivity of false ideas comes from knowing truth. And one will only know truth if he or she takes up daily residence in

God's Word. This is a must for each parent, church leader, and educator if we are going to be successful in renewing our minds.

One of the most challenging statements I have read in recent years was something that Kyle Idleman wrote in his book, *Gods at War*. There is only one place in this book where Idleman referred to the power of a worldview. He was relating to his readers the account of Joshua's closing address to Israel.

When Joshua knew that his life was coming to a close, he called the leaders of the nation together and gave them a final challenge. After reviewing all the amazing things God had done for Israel, Joshua told the people that it was time for them to make a decision. This decision was going to be the most important decision that they would ever make.

It was a decision to choose a god and follow that god. Joshua gave the people three choices (I guess one can say that a multiple-choice test is biblical!). One choice was for the people to go back to Egypt and follow the false gods their forefathers had followed. The second choice was to simply find the false gods right there in their own communities and follow them. Of course, the third option Joshua presented to the people was that they could be like him and choose to follow the true God of Israel. At this point, Idleman makes two powerful statements:

> *It's time to select a god and follow him!*
> **It's time to accept a worldview and let it remake you![55]**

---

55   Kyle Idleman, gods at War, Zondervan, 2013, p. 56

This same challenge is set before each of us today. It is time to choose a biblical worldview and let it remake us. It must start with us, not with our children and youth! After we repent of our sin and begin to renew our minds so that we develop a biblical worldview, we must address the issue of education biblically. It is not about where our children go to school. It is about providing our children and youth with a biblical worldview education at home, church, and school.

Too often when this has been attempted in the past, people have tried to change how they educated their children by simply modifying the systems and processes already in place. Let me share some examples of what I mean by this statement. Professor Gordon Clark of Butler University was quoted by Frank Gaebelein in *The Pattern of God's Truth:*

> *...where such good things as "giving out tracts...holding fervent prayer meetings, going out on gospel teams, opening classes with prayer" are the accepted practice; yet the actual instruction is no more Christian than in a respectable secular school....The program is merely a pagan education with a chocolate covering of Christianity. And the pill, not the coating, works....the students are deceived into thinking that they have received a Christian education when as a matter of fact their training has been neither Christian nor an education...*[56]

---

56   Gordan Clark, quoted in Frank E. Gaebelein, *The Pattern of God's Truth: Problems of Integration in Christian Education.* (Chicago, IL: Moody Press, 1954), 17.

These are very harsh words, but they must be heard and heeded. Gaebelein also shared what Dr. Edwin Rian wrote about what he believed needed to take place in our educational systems:

> *A Christian theory of education is an exposition of the idea that Christianity is a world and life view and not simply a series of unrelated doctrines. Christianity includes all of life. Every realm of knowledge, every aspect of life, and every facet of the universe find their place and their answer within Christianity. It is a system of truth enveloping the entire world in its grasp.*[57]

Nancy Pearcey stresses the importance of this truth when she wrote,

> *Christianity no longer functions as a lens to interpret the whole of reality; it is no longer held as total truth....We have to insist on presenting Christianity as a comprehensive, unified worldview that addresses all of life and reality. It is not just religious truth but total truth.*[58]

Once we embrace the truth that Christianity is a *system of truth, a unified worldview that envelops the entire world in its grasp,* then we must begin the process of rethinking education from a biblical perspective. Again, Dr. Rian says it well:

---

57 Edwin Rian, quoted in Frank E. Gaebelein, *The Pattern of God's Truth: Problems of Integration in Christian Education.* (Chicago, IL: Moody Press, 1954), 17-18.

58 Nancy Pearcey, *Total Truth: Liberating Christianity from Its Cultural Captivity.* (Wheaton, IL: Crossway Books), 69, 111.

The present tendency in education to add religion to the courses of study is comparable to attaching a garage to a home. What the building of knowledge needs is not a new garage but a new foundation.[59]

Every individual Christian, every Christian home, every church, and every Christian school must fully understand Kingdom Education™. Then we must know, understand, and commit ourselves to putting these principles into practice in the home, church, and school. We may discover when trying to do this that education doesn't need a new addition but a whole new foundation.

In order to fully understand the biblical principles of education, I encourage every reader to read and complete the companion resource to this book. *Applying Kingdom Education: Following God's Instructions for Educating Future Generations* will provide you with a detailed study of each of the 14 biblical principles of Kingdom Education™. There are application questions and exercises you can complete for each principle that will assist you in fully understanding God's plan for educating future generations.

For the sake of future generations, we must not delay one more day. We must understand Kingdom Education™ and follow God's directions for educating future generations.

It is time to *act*! God is looking for individuals, homes, churches, and schools to be committed to advance God's Kingdom. That means we must:

---

59   Edwin Rian, quoted in Frank E. Gaebelein, 18.

- *Embrace His mission*: We are to be God's chosen instruments to draw nations (especially our children and youth) to Him.

- *Embody His name*: We must represent His nature and character to future generations.

- *Obey His Word*: We must have a brand of holiness and not only address the issue of education but obey the principles of Kingdom Education™ in our lives, homes, churches, and schools.

In the spirit of Kyle Idleman's challenge, I end with these words:

> *It is time for individuals, homes, churches, and schools to embrace Kingdom Education™, follow God's directions, and prepare future generations to think and act from a biblical worldview so that they will turn their world upside down for Jesus Christ.*

Made in the USA
Columbia, SC
21 June 2021

40782065R00065